池のほとり

花と歩んだ七十年

At Pondside
—Seventy Years in *Ikebana*

At Pondside — Seventy Years in Ikebana

First printing	April 10, 2017
Author	Sen'ei Ikenobo
Publisher	Masafumi Ikenobo
Published by	Nihon Kadosha Co., Ltd.
	Sanjo Sagaru, Karasuma, Nakagyo-ku, Kyoto, Japan 6048134
	Telephone: +81-75-221-2687 (Editorial)
	+81-75-223-0613 (Sales)
Translated by	Maki Yamamura (Kyo Awase Inc.)
Edited by	Nicholas Sutton (Kyo Awase Inc.)
Photography by	Naotatsu Kimura, Yoriko Uchimaki
Layout by	Eiji Hayakawa
Printed and bound by	Tosho Printing Co., Ltd.

©Sen'ei Ikenobo 2017 Printed in Japan

To our Readers

Sen'ei Ikenobo, the 45th Generation Ikenobo Headmaster, inherited the title of Headmaster in 1945 when World War II ended, and in 2015 celebrated 70 years holding this title. His life in *ikebana* has been dramatic, which is typically represented in his innovative and unique *ikebana* style during the rapid ongoing changes of the times. The book is composed of a well-selected 31 short chapters of essays on his past and future, with some special pictures from the times. The straightforward tone of his storytelling is filled with numerous profound messages and the rules of life that bring the readers to the core significance of *ikebana*.

Ikenobo, the origin of *ikebana*, is rooted at the "pondside" of the Rokkakudo Temple in central Kyoto where, over 1400 years ago, flowers were offered on the tops of the Buddhist altar. The messages from the Headmaster, who has been supporting this long history and tradition over the last 70 years, we believe, is an invaluable asset not only to the *ikebana* professionals but also to anyone who leads and guides young students.

This book was originally published on June 1, 2016 in Japanese, and has been receiving positive reviews through an increasing number of readers. Responding to earnest requests from our followers all over the world, let alone in western countries, we are proud to publish this great work in English. We sincerely hope that this book opens a door to global readers, giving them a chance to experience some of the philosophy of *ikebana* and its lining of traditions.

Nihon Kadosha Editorial Desk

About the Author

池坊専永　Sen'ei Ikenobo

Born in Kyoto in 1933, Sen'ei Ikenobo inherited the title of 45th Generation Ikenobo Headmaster at age 11, upon his father's sudden passing. After intensive training on Mt. Hiei, he assumed the position of Head Priest at the Shiunzan Chohoji Temple (Rokkaku-do). He graduated from Doshisha University in Kyoto.

Based on the tradition and spirit of *ikebana*, he introduced a new *ikebana* not dependent on previous forms, creating *Shoka Shimputai* and *Rikka Shimputai* to harmonize with contemporary life. Thus he opened up a new world of *ikebana*.

Actively pursuing international cross-cultural communication through *ikebana* and contributing to education and dissemination of *ikebana* inside and outside Japan, in 2006 he was awarded the Order of the Rising Sun, Gold Rays with Neck Ribbon, by the Government of Japan, for meritorious cultural contribution.

In 2015, he celebrated 70 years as Headmaster of Ikenobo.

Introduction

We have a small pond next to our Rokkakudo Temple, with no specific name. Everyone here refers to it as just "the pond". This pond is obviously the oldest pond in the vicinity of this temple. It must have seen the establishment of the Rokkakudo Temple as well as the origin of *ikebana* itself. Here in the temple, as it is not so large, I can always feel the presence of the pond.

Looking back, the pond has always been with me, and I have lived beside it. This pond should know every single thing about me, the smiles, woes, sighs, as well as my daily advancement and my efforts. If the pond could say something, what would it say about me? I would like to listen to it, if possible, just all alone in private.

Once born we all keep growing, which also means we find ourselves in a continuous state of change. Change has also been the case for *ikebana*. It has changed over and over according to the sensibilities of the times. No such change can, though, deform the essence of self, and of *ikebana*. It is because of a central core inside. Those who have a stable core are strong, and so beautiful, and it is true to tradition. Once there is a strong core, it will not waver in the presence of a huge shift.

As for the pond at Rokkakudo Temple, where Prince Shotoku was reported to have taken a ritual bath, everything started from here, The Rokkakudo Temple, and *ikebana*.

This is the cornerstone that has connected us in the flower world. By this pond, Ikenobo has been, and will continue to be cherishing its flowers and its spirits.

Ikenobo — The place by the pond.* Lucid and meaningful.

At pondside in Rokkakudo Temple,

Sen'ei Ikenobo

*The word "Ikenobo" means "a hut by a pond" in Japanese.

At Pondside
— *Contents* —

To our Readers 1

About the Author..2

Introduction..3

Infinity in the Minimal 10

Mask and Face 13

Flowers not to be "Arranged"..17

Perverse..21

Father's Garden..24

What Creates the Culture? 28

Questioning..32

Doubting the Model 36

Creation by Feet, not Hands..40

Culture by Head, Culture by Heart 44

New Breeze 47

Dignity 51

Learning from Ink Painting...55

Sign 59

Lead and Support 62

What Training Gave Me 66

Here Again 70

Respect for Another 74

Individuality 77

Temple with Swans 80

How Teachers Should Be 84

Beauty of Life 87

My Syria Report 91

Memory of My Sense 95

Milestone 100

Message from *Ayu* *103*

Keeping the Soil for *Ikebana* *107*

Knowing the Genuine Article 111

The Promise of the Flower Buds 116

Walking Together 120

My Wish 124

Shushoe (at Main Building of Rokkakudo Temple)
Picture taken on January 1, 2016

At Pondside
— Seventy Years in Ikebana —

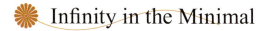 Infinity in the Minimal

Japanese beauty does not need much. Just like the garden of a Zen Buddhist temple, and like the acting in a *noh* performance, we Japanese are attracted to minimal act that can produce maximal result. In history, we have also experienced that sense of exquisite, luxurious beauty as we did in the 16th century, but in my understanding, Japanese always returns to a simple beauty in the end.

Being minimal, having nothing, and being simple. This does not necessarily mean paucity. For example, *haiku*, the shortest poetry in the world, can express numerous scenes just with 17 syllables*.

"*Suzumenoko Sokonoke Sokonoke Oumagatoru*"
(Watch out, little sparrows. A horse will come.)

Issa Kobayashi

Taking this *haiku* just as it is stated, the meaning is just simply an alert to the sparrows. We Japanese see much more than this however, because we imagine various situations derived from these brief words to gain much more information.

It tells us that the scene is during daytime, in summer, since the sparrow is a seasonal word indicating it is summertime, and the fact they are playing means it is daytime. A quiet, peaceful time it should be for a while, which Issa, the author has enjoyed. Maybe there are villages or bushes nearby where the sparrows live. Suddenly a horse is approaching with thundering noise. Issa cannot help telling the sparrows to run away soon. In this way a simple line of *haiku* hints at many more stories behind.

The Japanese believe, or rather seek for something invisible. They are the people who are not satisfied just by observing what is visible, simply because they are always looking for the way toward some truth or essence, which is often invisible. We tend to think, if we cannot see anything valuable in the invisible, then it is simply because we are not yet ready for it due to our immaturity or lack of virtue.

The more we try, the more we can access the truth that has not paraded itself before us—I think this is why Japanese like to dwell on the mysteries of the core, rather than just the surface decoration, through endless omission or deletion to the limit, moving toward the minimal core, which we believe to be a clear representation of the truth.

Ikebana, or *kado*, also aims at the world of doing "*-do*," the way, just as in "*budo*" or "*sado*." We imagine ourselves participating in the lives of flowers, trying to find the truth. To do this, we omit a number of branches or leaves so that we can concentrate on the lives of plants. A good representative of this is a piece of single camellia blossom, the traditional Ikenobo *ikebana*. The magnificent tree of camellia will be displayed in the sincerest form of minimalism, three and a half leaves, and a single flower.

If either of this limited number of leaves or the flower is missing, or unbalanced, it does not come to life anymore, it is just a lifeless branch. The traditional Ikenobo *ikebana* requires us to learn omission, to the limit.

Omitting as much as possible and still giving an impression of living green life. Letting the minimal bring the maximum, limitless effect. This should also be what we aim for in our own lives.

---

*Haiku, the Japanese poetic form, traditionally consists of 17 *on* (also known as morae though often loosely translated as "syllables"), in three phrases of 5, 7, and 5 on respectively.

Mask and Face

We all have many faces with us. You could be a child and parent, husband or wife, and the one running a business at the same time, using a suitable face according to the situation. I also have many "faces" I carry with me, but my official face should be the one of Headmaster, and Head priest of Rokkakudo Temple. When we are not ready to take on a position or title, either because of immaturity or being mentally unprepared, we have no "face" but rather we carry a makeshift "mask" instead.

Perhaps we wear such masks until we eventually come to own our own true and sure face. I also wore such a mask a long time ago.

During my elementary school days I carried the face of just a child, without any title, specifically until I reached 11 years of age, around the time when my father passed away. I knew that my father had been the Head priest, and so too was my grandfather, but I was too childish to recognize the whole meaning of that, the responsibilities and expectations that a Headmaster should have.

Still amid the grief after my father's passing, my surroundings drastically changed. I found myself dispatched to a temple in Sakamoto, in the Hiei foothills, where my ascetic training to be a monk suddenly started. I was totally confused, not knowing any reasons for what I was being told to do.

Training and practice, such as reading sutras or learning manners as a monk, were nothing but difficult to me as a child. I felt uneasy, even though I looked reasonable as a monk with my head shaved and wearing a monk's gown. My sutra reading was of course terrible and my manners were just following someone else's. Obviously, I was just a child with the mask of a monk, who could not yet acquire the real face for it.

Many might think I should have been more thoroughly trained in *ikebana* than anything, since I was born as the eldest son of an Ikenobo Headmaster. But the reality was not like that. Training to be monk was the priority, because an Ikenobo Headmaster should be the one to inherit the vocation of Rokkakudo Head priest first. Two years or so later I started *ikebana* training, which is only incorporated when one is already training to be a monk.

Gradually, my days in the temple became days filled with enthusiasm, and ten years later I started to acquire the face of a monk, instead of that awkward mask of a monk I had been wearing. I was twenty years old at that time, and this was when I was sufficiently qualified to be the Head priest of Rokkakudo Temple after the Shinzanshiki, the inauguration ceremony for new head priests.

Being twenty years old, and having completed the harsh training of a monk, I was ready and confident enough to aim for the next step, that is, to become a Headmaster of Ikenobo, prepared to thoroughly work out my way into the future. All of my training days in the temple gave me the state of mind that I would accept the "face" of a monk and at the same time, the "face" of a Headmaster. Although the people around me might have thought I had a slightly shaky start because of my young age, I think at that time I had already seen the face of the Headmaster that I myself should have in my future.

Shinzanshiki ceremony (October 1953): The author is second from the head.

Flowers not to be "Arranged"

How do you think *ikebana* should be expressed in English? Flower arrangement might be the name that comes to mind, but actually we do not "arrange" flowers. In Japanese, there are a couple of verbs for when performing "*ikebana*," like "*sasu*," to put or arrange, and "*ikeru*," the latter I believe is the right one. Some may find no difference between the two, but I would say not. Let me explain the difference.

The verb "*sasu*" in Japanese uses the Chinese characters whose meanings are manual operations such as inserting or pointing out. On the other hand, the verb "*ikeru*" uses the characters whose meanings are related to life, or activity —something strongly related to life. Briefly, "*sasu*" means actions, and "*ikeru*" means life.

The reason why I discriminate between these two words is because in the *ikebana* of Ikenobo, the ultimate beauty roots in the life of greenery. "*Sasu*" can be nothing different from just randomly throwing flowers into a bucket of water. On the other hand, "*ikeru*" means something like considering the lives of flowers. Just as we think of others, we think of greenery and flowers. How they have been living so far and in what environment; do they like light or do they rather prefer shade?—Not just the shapes of flowers or leaves, which is visibly clear, but what we should always care about is rather how the plant has been fairing up to now, which may not be visibly apparent.

According to the introduction of "Ikenobo Sen'no Kuden" (Oral Instruction by Ikenobo Sen'no), which states the most essential spirit of Ikenobo *ikebana*, our flowers should be based on the "beauty of the original impression given to us by each plant." *

The "original impression" here does not mean a shape or a form of the real entity of flowers, but rather the ideal image of the plant including the history of its life. In other words, the ancestor of Ikenobo tried to overlap the image of people to that of flowers, to seek the way for us to live. This is a specific artistic expression unique to Japan, called "*mitate*" (analogy).

Lilies headed to the ground refer to pureness, plums blooming amid the chill refer to patience, and bamboos standing forward refer to straightforwardness. They sought to consider our own situations or characters when observing the plants and their own properties. Why—just for learning more in our lives. To learn this, the plants should be alive. They should not be flowers only in shape, nor leaves or branches to be focused on, but the whole plant considered as a living body should be there. We therefore should express this as "*ikeru*" in Japanese which means make the plants live.

Not only are flowers in bloom beautiful. Beauty is the life that made it happen. The life of plants, is the very root of the beauty cherished by Ikenobo, the identity.

* "The beauty of the original impression given to us by each plant": The original Japanese is "*Yoroshiki Omokage.*"

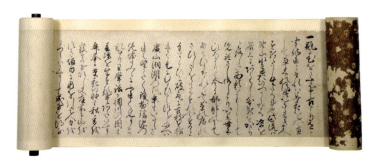

"Ikenobo Sen'no Kuden," which hands down the Ikenobo spirit.
(Manuscript copied in 1537)

 Perverse

When many choose red, I would rather choose a different color. I tend to view things at another angle, looking from below when others without doubt would naturally look at the front. I like such a snap or twist in every way. Perhaps I am a little perverse myself.

Everything has a front, top side, or a normal perspective. Typical examples are the pictures we see in a pictorial book, where the pictures are taken from a conventional point of view. Giraffes are always taken with their long neck, and tulips are shown from their side, not from the top, so that each characteristic can be emphasized.

If I were to take pictures, however, I want the ones that are a unique composition or leave a unique impression, where even though such pictures cannot be easily recognized, people would surely understand once given a hint. Simple beautiful pictures do not satisfy someone irrational like me. Rather, I would be thrilled by surprising someone and hearing comments like "Oh really? Was it?" or "That was the last thing I noticed."

Of course, if such shock or surprise is just too much so as not to be understood by anyone, it is just a self-complacency. If, on the other hand, such surprise is completely read beforehand, it would be just beneath the dignity of the perverse. Being correctly perverse is not easy.

This is why I observe things, to catch even a slightest new change. This does not bother me as I have been fond of observing things at length since my younger days. Sometimes watching things for a while makes me find an unexpectedly beautiful image in them. Such an image or impression may not be suitable for a pictorial book, but even so, it may touch my heart more than anything else.

Such findings are the ones to which my *ikebana* works are greatly indebted. Shop windows of department stores, an object in a museum, a line of ants, a stack of fallen leaves, the path of light through a window, and the Moon or stars seen from between the trees—accumulations of such small sparkling moments in life impresses upon my later works directly or indirectly.

Observation is always important for everything. First we need a close look from a general point of view. Based on that, an independent standpoint is to be added. This is the time for me to become perverse, trying to be different from others. This helps me to encounter something "true," such as shining beauty or a breathtaking surprise. This is what a perverse person like me desires to have.

This process is just like the shift of practice process from *Shofutai* to *Shimputai*. We first practice *Shofutai* which has a certain model many times over. While practicing the model, we observe countless branches and flowers, and sometimes encounter unexpectedly an impressive look of them lined by beauty or strength, even though such a look is not applicable to the rule of *Shofutai* model. Through such experience, our own unique sensitivity toward plants is refined. This would then lead to *Shimputai* which has no model to depend on, but treats the encounter of our unique sensitivity to the plants.

Taking a close look seems to be a roundabout approach. Yet sometimes it is a good idea to go such a long way round, taking along your inner perverse feeling. That is my recommendation.

Father's Garden

My garden has innumerable plants. You may think the garden of the Headmaster of Ikenobo must be a gorgeous Japanese garden that a landscape gardener constantly endeavors to perfect. Yet this garden, which my father designed, is not like that at all. Rather, this is a place where plants rule all, and the variety of plants is spontaneously growing. I trim them only when they disturb the neighbors.

"No more *ikebana!*"

I used to dare to cry out when I was a child. This should have brought my father to his wits' end, but he didn't show it, nor did he force me to practice *ikebana*. Perhaps he knew what my reaction would be against his persuasion, besides he actually wanted me to voluntarily develop my interest. So instead of teaching me *ikebana*, my father told me various interesting stories about the flowers or trees planted in our garden at every possible opportunity.

"If we have Bamboo, we are safe if earthquakes decide to come because of its extensive roots."

"Gingko trees are succulent enough to protect us in the event of fire."

"A camphor tree's minty smell works as an insect repellent."

"Camellia cleverly stows its buds under its leaves during the cold season."

"The roots of peony are like those of trees, but its flowers are like those of plants."

As such, he told much about flowers, and about trees. It might have been his strategy toward a reluctant son, to bring about even a small botanical impression which just might lead to *ikebana* in some way. However the result was that I was soon held captive by his stories, as I was naturally very fond of observation.

Looking back, I am sure my father fully intended to teach me the natural essence of the various species, and the colorful styles and stories of their lives, through this garden.

He went away when he was just forty-four years old. I was only eleven, in the final grade at elementary school. It was just out of expectation for him, let alone for many other people surrounded. I missed the opportunity to learn *ikebana* technique directly from my father because he passed away so suddenly, but more than that, he taught me the life and spirit of trees and flowers. In such a way he opened the way to one day becoming a Headmaster in my distant future as it seemed then.

Standing before the trees that I used to look at and study with my father, I am strongly convinced of this.

What Creates the Culture?

Ikebana is a culture. So I have pointed out many times in interviews or in my books. Some of you might have already heard I said so. When we look up the word "culture" in a dictionary, it roughly leads us to a concept of "everything, either tangible or intangible, that humans create on their own" in addition to the complex explanation. What attracts me is the phrase, "humans create on their own."

There are countless lives on the Earth, but only humans can create an object. It is the difference between animals and humans, the former live simply with their bodies gifted from heaven, but the latter creates something to wear if it is too cold, and builds a house for protection from wind and rain. Moreover, they are not satisfied by merely creating them. Once created, they pursue warmer clothes, more resilient houses, and further, more beautiful clothes and more comfortable houses.

You may say some animals would also make their nests. Of course they do make nests, but this is from their natural instincts. They do not seek for decoration of their nests nor change the nests' style according to the era.

Humans, like animals, with the instinct of living or preserving species, have been said to seek "Truth, goodness, and beauty." As we humans have been seeking truth, laying out an ideal of goodness, and adoring beauty, we have ended up in a position of creating cultures and watching them develop.

As I stated at the beginning, *ikebana* is also a culture. Perhaps long ago before *ikebana* came into the world, or in its early stages, I imagine people merely loved the beauty of the flowers. When they tried to find the basis of flowers' attractiveness, they found that it was part of the plants' vital functions at last, which in turn opened a door of ideology to the culture of *ikebana*. Thus, I understand that a culture "matures" when it has multiple derivations from multiple doors opened from a single source. In this context, the culture of *ikebana* should be a highly matured culture of beauty, growing from a seed that evaluates a beautiful flower, opening doors to Truth that teach the natural life cycles, and to goodness that allow us to show hospitality for our guests through flowers.

We have in our hands the means by which we can nurture and develop what we have created. Then why cannot we be hungrier for something more true, better, and more beautiful?

Tanabata Rikka kai (Flower exhibition at the Star Festival) in Rokkakudo Temple around 1700 ("Hoei Karaku Saiken-zu" published in 1704)

 Questioning

As I come across things of interest while I travel, I like to set up questions for myself and seek answers, like why an object has acquired such an interesting shape, or how it came to be placed in a certain location. This is possibly come due to my experience of frequently replying to various questions that arise in my work and during the many interviews I have had. I always try to properly explain the logic of matters by obtaining a full understanding or background. Simply, I am interested in the stories that hide behind objects which I can explain and which ultimately make complete sense, and such stories also add ever more joy and color to my memory of the places I have visited.

This is why I tend to refer to some meaning when placing or decorating any of the things I like to have around me.

For example, carp in the ponds of the Rokkakudo precinct as well as on the first floor of the Ikenobo building are only either gold, silver, or black in color. People generally imagine Asian carp of red and white, but I chose only those of gold, silver, and black. I selected them because flowers in nature usually have no such color. This is the place for us to do *ikebana* every day. My intention is to let every single element play a single role of supporting the natural flowers we use for *ikebana*. Whatever parts are colorful should be preserved only for flowers.

On the trees in the precinct, or the roof of the hall you can see several ornaments of a horned owl. I heard many saying it would be a sign of good fortune when one has found all of the owls. Since I like owls myself, some seem to believe that I placed these ornaments from my sense of fun. Actually this is not so. I put these ornaments in the places I wanted to deter the pigeons. This may sound too practical and rather uninteresting but nevertheless it is true.

Also beside the grand staircase on the first floor lobby of the Ikenobo building I placed a series of elephants made of wood wholly sculpted from a single tree. Numbers of elephants make a line, and we can enjoy the process of carving in this artwork where the rough cutting in the rearmost elephant gradually changes through the line toward precision work at the front. I found this carving when I visited Thailand, and as I first saw this work I realized what constituted training and discipline. The path from an immature style of *ikebana* is refined by practice, a slow-but-steady training path that trainees pursue, the one to go ahead, the one to follow, an endless and continuous *ikebana* path—such images are well depicted and implied by the elephants. The carving is displayed with a passage from "Ikenobo Sen'no Kuden";

"Even with little talent, as long as you train with persistence, you can eventually establish a form with taste and beauty."

If we are not conscious enough, everything we see in our world, each event in front of our eyes just passes by without any meaning. We should not passively receive what is then there but should always question "why." And we should have our own view based on the knowledge gained by reasoning. Such an attitude of treating both sides of the matter should always assist us when we are sitting before the plants.

Wood carving of elephants in the Ikenobo building

Doubting the Model

The tea ceremony, *"noh," "budo,"* and *"kabuki"*— Japanese cultural traditions often have a "model" to follow. Of course, *ikebana* has one too. In *Ikenobo, Rikka*, which has been handed down from the *Muromachi* era, and *Shoka*, which was established in the latter half of the *Edo* era, have models known as *"Shofutai."* The model is in a way the fusion of a sophisticated sense of beauty refined by successive generations of Headmaster and the practical use of it. This specific sophisticated sense of beauty is well represented in the rule of 7-5-3 syllables, lighting in *"tokono-ma,"* and the relationship between *"kamiza"* and *"shimoza."*

As the basic structure of *ikebana* is obtained by positioning the *"yakueda"* according to the model, the model is quite useful in showing a sample to beginners. Elementary practices start by training with this model a number of times. I myself used to learn models to attain competency according to them.

However, as I have taken numerous types of greenery and flowers in my hands, a notion came up in my mind. Everything is judged by the model, but should it be? I should cut and remove this plum branch of a very unique expression, once it is out of the model. Even a flower expressing some special aura is simply refused by the model, which was hard for me to understand. Such an uncomfortable feeling has been haunting me even as I worked to complete beautiful works through strict adherence to the model given to me.

Vegetables and fruits in the fields are eaten by birds and insects in the order of excellence of their taste. Birds and insects do not hesitate to take what they prefer, as they should know it by their instincts and experiences. And this should be the same with plants should it not? While we are so attracted to a piece of a branch in front of us, how can we merely brush it aside?

Of course I do not mean to deny the model. I have seen the beauty of the model, and I am confident and proud of this Ikenobo tradition. Still, being the Headmaster of *ikebana*, I have started questioning the model at the same time. I felt frustration and confusion so that the more I pursued the model the more I lost the colorful individuality, which in turn could hinder my devotion of putting my soul into the flowers. I just could not give up the beauty I was truly impressed by simply because of the model restriction. This was tantamount to lying to myself. I realized my resolute desire to represent the natural beauty of greenery which moved my heart, even though I had no idea of how I could do this, seeking the beauty out of only the model, amid the model-oriented *ikebana* world. Obviously, this was the story before I created the style of "*Shimputai*."

Creation by Feet, not Hands

The garden produced by my father was rather an "environment" simulating the natural world rather than an elaborate garden. A tiny waterfall, selaginella in the shade, tree peony and alpine rose—it is something far from the normal concept of a "garden." As described in "Father's Garden," I unconsciously gained so much knowledge from this garden just by being in it.

Branches and flowers in the garden cut out from the natural scenery is the origin forme. This greenery is not "well-tamed." It stretches its branches everywhere trying to find sunlight. Those parts that love shade try to establish themselves in shadowy areas. Even though planting pretty fringed iris in a sunny area, it would rather grow into the shade soon in the next season. Surrounded by such spontaneous plants, I was naturally brought up with the conviction that they essentially push through their lives by their own intentions.

One day I saw a flower growing in a greenhouse, which gave me a very strange feeling. The flower was just too quiet, despite my expectations. It did not say anything to me, and I felt nothing with that flower. I tried to figure out the reason of this. What is the difference between the natural greenery and the plants in a greenhouse?

The greenhouse was conditioned to be an appropriate temperature. It assured sufficient nutrition and water. Everything seemed to be just perfect. Of course there was enough air but wait a minute—the air was still, with no breeze—I realized ....

When I was young, I visited Tsuruga in Fukui prefecture which was the hometown of my mother. In summer we used to go swimming to Matsubara park. I was just a teenager and astonished by the beauty of the pine trees lining the coast. What made these pine trees so majestic?

The trunks of pine trees bend towards the inland side due to the strong shore winds, and then bend back toward the sea. Seemingly unstable, they stand in a perfect balance. Why does this happen?

Through consideration, I found an answer in their roots that are resistant to the harsh sea winds, and the wind that worked too much in developing their trunks and roots. What moved me was actually this invisible power and existence of the wind. I was impressed by nothing but the beauty and strength of the pine trees enduring the wind. As plants cannot move away from their rooted place, they have no choice but staying to live their lives under the given environment. How harsh it may be, they need to accept and hold on to their lives by all means. Such effort should be the one to move me, and many more.

In cities, people might have a limited chance of seeing flowers, such as in flower shops and greenhouses. There some flowers are prepared by carefully removing their leaves, or there are others that are available all through the year, which causes us to feel less and less seasonal sensitivity. This all makes it difficult for us to understand the real life of the plants. What was their original form? Where and how do they grow? Do they love shade or watersides? When do they bloom and what kind of seeds they have? People in the past used to say, "Do *ikebana* by using your feet." Just because the knowledge we indirectly gain through books or media compared to knowledge attained through actual experience is totally different.

We may complete a work beautiful in its shape, even without knowing the life of the flowers from which it is made. But I do not doubt that the more deeply we know their lives, the more firmly we can grasp the brightness of their lives. I believe, watching their true existence crystalizes inspiration.

Culture by Head, Culture by Heart

We always request abundance, comfort, and beauty. From this, many cultures were born, and excellent cultures have been handed down over the years. I think, such cultures created and developed by people can be roughly classified into a "culture of the head" and a "culture of the heart."

Development of the former has been continuously making our social lives more and more convenient. Taking the advantages of this, so our lives are very comfortable. We get abundant information from TV, and communicate with anyone wherever we are thanks to mobile phones. Airplanes and bullet trains enable rapid transportation over long distances, and technology allows humans to even venture into space. And then computers came into our lives. Now we are almost unconscious of any time gap between foreign countries, through the development and enhancement of computers. The culture of the head has dramatically advanced beyond our expectations over the last hundred years or so.

On the other hand, the culture of the heart has been nursing our souls, and has enriched us in our spirits. Typically represented by art, like paintings, sculptures, music, and drama, as well as religious faith. *Ikebana* that Ikenobo has been long handing down belongs to the culture of the heart.

While the culture of the head makes our lives convenient, the culture of the heart makes our spirits rich and colorful. Even while seeking beauty or joy, our lives are not only filled with happy and joyful things. Even with the advancements of science and technology, distress, grief, fear and anger never ends. The culture of the heart can act on such a state of our minds.

The culture of the head depends on letters and numerical values to pass it on, while to convey the culture of the heart we must depend on our feelings and senses, such as eyesight, hearing, smell, taste, and touch, as well as the sensitivity to perceive them. Due to our natural inclinations, usually we are only comfortable with one or the other of these "cultures." Yet between the two neither is superior.

Because both cultures can develop based on the coexistence of logical thinking and the completeness of sensitivity.

However, nowadays especially the culture of the head, has seen remarkable advances, and people tend to think that this is the only versatile solution to the problems we have. It is very difficult to express the value and legacy of the culture of the heart in quantified terms, and it would end in quite a superficial outcome if we were to try to do so.

Ikebana incorporates expressions brought by each flower, feeling for seasons, and harmony with the space, all of which encounter with the intention of the creator. It has no meaning to accurately measure the length of flower to simulate a superb *ikebana* work. Numbers are meaningless in this case. Rather, we need to see it with our own eyes, and move our own hands to obtain the essence of the work. To experience the culture of the heart, as in the saying of seeing is believing, we must work our own senses and soul.

# New Breeze

Throughout our history, our successive Headmasters have been creating new flower models and structures and incorporating them into their style. I also aimed to incorporate some new ideas. I announced *Shoka Simputai* in 1977, and *Rikka Shimputai* in 1999. Both styles have released the restrictions long maintained to simply and honestly express the inspiration received from the plants without complete reliance on the models. This must be a dramatic event to Ikenobo which has long held dear these traditional models.

Looking at my past works, I found myself feeling rather uncomfortable following *Shofutai*. There, "*yakueda*" was expressed more by indication rather than through the model, resulting in work that is sometimes difficult to comprehend. I never intended to undervalue the model, but the approach of "spreading out" of the model has become the basis of my works.

Before announcing *Shoka Shimputai*, I was struggling to find my way of expression, repeating numerous trials to find something I was sure of. And when the time came finally, I had a meeting with the seior professors of Ikenobo, the then major players among us.

Although expected to some extent, I saw the weight of the established. They said, "We have a great model, which has been cherished over the years. Following the model is Ikenobo's rule. What you're doing is stepping over it, which is what you should *not* do."

Being the Headmaster, I was still very young at that time, at least compared to the senior professors. Still, I was prepared and determined. I was so eager to directly express the movement I had received from the impression of plants, but just without the filter of the model. Only because I believed that the power of *ikebana* could represent the beauty of flowers and branches from a different perspective than the beauty that the models alone could convey. I confronted the opposition of the professors, persuaded them, and eventually attained an opportunity to announce the *Shoka Simputai*.

Now about 40 years have passed since then, and nearly 20 years have passed since *Rikka Shimputai*, too. There are many *Shimputai* works in the exhibitions. This makes me realize that so far, the new sensitivity of beauty in *ikebana* has gained acceptance.

This is not only a story for *ikebana*. Our sense at a particular time cannot stop changing. For example, clothing. How do we see it if we in the present day are wearing the clothing of the generation of our mothers or grandmothers? Colors and patterns fabulous in those days would be somewhat differently taken in the modern age. It is the matter of sense that plays a big role. Similarly, *ikebana* should also accommodate the age. The *Shimputai*'s brilliant growth should demonstrate its success in harmonization with our era.

Shimputai itself cannot be exempt from change. Compared to the time when it was originated, the current *Shimputai* has been changing quite a lot. A sense of the times is something like this. I can even imagine a day when *Shimputai* itself will fade away. If it is good enough to last, it will, and if not, it won't. Nothing more than that. I would rather stick to an attitude of being open-minded and ready for such a change.

In the long history of Ikenobo, my tenure is like the blink of an eye. Perhaps numerous styles have been pursued, some of which must have already vanished. Still, those who live in the modern age are responsible for creating the modern *ikebana* styles, with the values and the excellence being handed on to the next generations.

Techniques to uphold the tradition, and the flexibility to feel various new values and to incorporate them. Where these seemingly opposite elements get together, a chemical reaction occurs to generate works that fit in with the times... only because the new breeze never stops.

# Dignity

Do you know that the tulips that bring spring to gardens do not grow naturally in tropical countries? Tulips put forth their buds and stretch their leaves in spring after spending a severe winter as bulbs. On the other hand, bulbs which have been put into a refrigerator to simulate this hibernation that are then grown in a greenhouse sprout into a slim shape, which looks quite different from those grown in the wild.

Tropical plants with relaxed and easygoing characters are charming, but personally I am attracted by plums blooming in a chill, or pine trees rooting against ocean air. Simply because of their braveness and fortitude that struggles in a severe natural environment to bloom just one more flower, to stretch just one more branch.

The beauty that our heart senses through the plants is a beauty endorsed by the background environment of those plants. This is in a way a type of beauty that can make sense to spiritual minds. An appreciation that requires prior knowledge and observation. Such beauty that inspires the innermost spirit should be endowed with "dignity."

Generally speaking, dignity refers to nobleness or grace, an aura from within the personality or character. The dignity of Ikenobo *ikebana* must dwell on a sensitivity for beauty based on the natural essence of each plant. On which land a plant has rooted, and how it fairs as it grows—such backgrounds are eloquent enough for those who are willing to know them to catch their message, without misleading through superficial shape, form, or color.

Interestingly, *ikebana* works reflect the dignity of the one whose work it is. Through the work, just as so in the flowers and branches, we are actually looking into the author's mind alongside shape, form, or color.

We can discern a person's dignity from various situations, as in the person's behavior or use of language, and belongings. The appearance of floral shears can also tell so much about their owner. Worn handles show the accumulation of the practices the owner has, and the dirty state of the shears also chances to expose an attitude.

Furthermore, dignity is invisible to those who do not understand it, so simulation means nothing. In other words, plants of dignity cannot necessarily add any of it to the work.

In Ikenobo *ikebana*, the part just away from the water surface, which is free from any leaves or small branches, is called as "*mizugiwa*." *Mizugiwa* should be always clearly organized, without gaps, twists, or skewing of the stem branches. Of course this is also from the authentic reason that such work with a poor state of *mizugiwa* impairs the visual level of completion, but more than this we stick to the beauty of *mizugiwa* because we believe it is the core basis of the plants' life. It is just like the shoes of a dressed-up lady that are marked or when her manner is improper. This can eventually damage the beautiful clothing and even her personality; such a simple thing can actually affect the entirety. Appearance does not mean everything, yet even appearance can reveal much enough about the inner workings.

So, I hope especially that the masters lead their disciples to be people of dignity. I hope that they keep pushing forward to their goals of life with will, rather than spending days without purpose. A well-organized work can be attained to some extent by daily practices, but to create a work that touches one's heart, we must discipline our minds. Furthermore, I hope that they come to possess the proper manners to grow as models for younger generations.

This is not an easy task of course. But in the same way that we are moved by the plants embracing their lives, so those sincerely facing their lives ahead of them attract our attention as they move us with their endeavors. Such attitudes will surely lighten the path of *ikeban*a, and so the many successors will follow.

Learning from Ink Painting

Besides my father, I had another teacher who was conversant with botany and taught me much about it. He was a teacher to teach me ink painting when I was a high school student.

He came to my house once a week to teach me ink painting. We did not draw, write or paint using a desk as support, but placed the paper on a felt carpet spread on the *tatami* floor matting. Initially I tried to draw following closely the way my teacher worked.

As you may know, ink paintings are usually drawn using ink only. No other colors are used but instead only ink contrast, density and blurring are used to express a great variety of tints of color. Unlike color painting, ink painting completely relies on the gradation of a single base color.

I first learned how to paint orchids, bamboos, chrysanthemums, and plums in this way. One of the techniques I learned was that when drawing the leaves of an orchid, I needed to just drop the brush onto a point on the paper, and then move the brush in a certain way without hesitation. Leaves should not be drawn with a uniform density, but rather with an extreme light shade, rapidly darkening only at the very end of the brush stroke. This brilliantly expresses the delicate nuances of back/front, positive and negative ("*in-yo*") of the leaves. I remember my teacher used to moisten the point of the brush with his tongue, slightly diluting the ink to obtain subtly lighter shades.

When painting bamboo, my teacher used to say, "Do not draw the bamboo from the top, since it grows from the root. Its power dwells in its roots, which is what pushes it skyward." He would draw bamboo trees while saying this, turning his brush sideways and strongly moving it from the bottom to the top to draw the bamboo joints, and suddenly there before me would be a formidable bamboo tree standing firm in the ground. He taught me not only how I should move my brush but also particular features unique to each of the many varieties of plants and trees I learned to paint as well.

Even now, so much later, I still sometimes refer to many drawings when I find a perfect tree or flower for my *ikebana* work. Why do I do this? Well, because of the excellent compositions that can be found made by professional artists. They have superb compositional skills that contain the target in a frame. Furthermore the drawings, especially ink paintings, allow one to easily discern the important features within each target.

Unlike ink paintings, I was never taught calligraphy by anyone. As I have experienced many occasions of writing my own and other people's names using brushes, I have practiced it on my own, by referring to a calligraphy publication that I bought in China that concentrates on a particular technique. This book contains many styles for a single character, and from this I acquired some of my favorite styles on my own. I practiced over and over, copying my favorite style until I finally mastered it. When doing this, my skills gained from my ink painting classes with my teacher, including how to move my brush, helped me a lot. Perhaps it is because I had learned basic brush control from ink painting that now some even say that my handwritten characters using a brush look like paintings!

"Meditation" written and drawn by Sen'ei Ikenobo

 Sign

I definitely deny certain ideas that doubt the existence of something invisible. However, I feel I must point out that this is not a story about Hogwarts. This is about aesthetics that are specific to the Japanese people.

When you imagine some Japanese paintings on "*kakejiku*" or "*fusuma*" for instance, there must be some empty space besides the main depictions of characters, animals, or plants. This empty space does not represent a void, and it does not imply a notion of incompleteness or that the artist was negligent in some way. Compared to this, in western paintings, I suppose the raw canvass exposed would not be so popular. The canvass would be filled in with something that might include tiny details in the background or with just some color. On the other hand, the Japanese approach includes an attempt to instill some sign, hinting at the empty parts and pronouncing them as a part of the work. Trying to see this invisible something that has been instilled, requires a mind predisposed to such a sense of beauty.

In Japanese culture, blank space is not the monopoly of paintings. Traditional Japanese beauty is perceived when it embraces clear space in some way. In gardens we can see such space arising from the arrangement of stones, or between stone and wood. In *noh*, the performers usually take time (*"ma"*) during their varied pace of movement. And so it is with *ikebana*, too. Between the branches we require both density and space. Gardens, *noh*, and *ikebana* commonly try to express the same Japanese aesthetics, one of which manifests itself as blank areas or regions containing nothing.

Since *ikebana* usually uses symmetrical composition, there are some spaces between each branch whether large or small. These spaces by definition, play an important role in *ikebana* works just as their equivalents do Japanese paintings.

We *ikebana* creators sense a variety of natural scenes in this space; imagining for instance, moonlight, feeling the wind moving across, and hearing the sounds of insects when finding a disfigured leaf. Thus we see something invisible, we hear something inaudible. Further we try to incorporate the path of life that this plant has had, where it emerged and how it grew.

It may sound a little esoteric to some, but I believe most of us should have a sense that enables us to "see" something invisible. When seeing a religious figure for example, some of us might naturally have that sense of awe even without being told so. That sense of awe comes not from the actual shape of such a figure, but rather from the sign of endless energy and power inside that can be sensed in every part of such a figure, such as in the fingers, neck, or eyes. Such sensitivity is what I pursue in order to refine, for better expression of such invisible but potentially meaningful signs in *ikebana*.

Mind, or heart is something everyone should firmly possesses inside, although no one can actually see or touch it. Such an invisible mind or heart, one can envisage, might attain an ability to "see" something invisible, and "hear" something inaudible. I am sure these aesthetics are somewhat specific to the Japanese people and are the precious foundations that support this aspect of Japanese culture. Indeed, precious enough to hand on to future generations.

❋ Lead and Support

Let alone monodrama, usually on the stage, traditional or contemporary, there are some players together. Performances by lead roles are wonderful as expected, drawing the audience into the story. Sometimes there are a number of actors in lead roles, which is really an interesting experience, with their powerful and continuous dialogs, but personally I feel overwhelmed by such a large helping of dramatic discourse.

I rather prefer a distinct difference between the lead role and the support roles. I prefer that the support roles always project the lead role—promoting on the stage. Especially in *kabuki*, the lead role appears only in limited highlights of the story, and soon disappears. Through the lead's fleeting appearance by design, the stage is filled with an afterglow, so as to surely make the audience miss him. So it is that the support roles accentuate the audience's sense of loss.

In *ikebana*, we use terms that equate to lead or major roles and support roles. Specifically, the major role is major material and support roles are support materials, where the former is the flowers or branches that the creator would be attracted to, and the latter is the other flowers and branches all of which are components of the entire work. You may think, to highlight the major role (or material), the rest of the piece would simply consist of those basic supporting flowers or branches that are less impressive. Surprisingly perhaps, this is not actually so. Even among the supporting materials, each has its own character, which acts as an agent to augment the personality of the major role (or material), all of which should be integrated into a completed harmonized artwork.

This reminds me of the relationships between actors on the stage. It is of course the lead role that wins attention, which is however not the point in the entire context. The charms of the lead role come about through the colors of the supporting roles, and what fleshes out the story is the movement, the lines of the supporting roles, the chemistry of which combines to create a stimulating landscape. There is no need to heat up the stage constantly, and there is no need for all the players to be ostentatious. If any scene lasts in the audience's memory when the final curtain falls, it simply means it was a good play. Just like music that brings a rich melody—it is accompanied by carefully chosen changes in volume and tempo.

Looking back to *ikebana*, there is no rule for placing the major material and the support materials in the work. Some *ikebana* schools use many flowers, including the major and the support, so some may even prefer no clear distinction between the major and the supporting roles. Further, a single branch of a rose in a bud vase can be complete as is, in its beauty, requiring nothing else.

Still, I would emphasize that precious moment familiar to me in which a single flower encounters with another single branch only, to generate a beauty greater than the sum of its isolated parts. In our *Shoka Shimputai*, the branch corresponding to *"shu"* (major) is known as *"yo"* (support), and with another branch called as *"ashirai"* which assists or coordinates the above two, all these three elements (*"shu," "yo," and "ashirai"*) are used to express numerous sentiments or backgrounds. Whether the combination of the three can move the viewer depends on the appreciative and expressive ability of the creator.

I believe the relationship of the major role and the support role to be reciprocal and they should always be paired, complementing each other like light and shadow. A part of a piece which is not illuminated does not mean it has no use in the whole work; it is the shadow which is also necessary for the other parts to win the light. The major part is here because the support is there, on the stage, and in *ikebana* it is the same.

What Training Gave Me

In September 1945, I entered the Buddhism priesthood in Shoren-in Temple at Awataguchi, Kyoto. It was when I was 12 years old, four months after I lost my father, one month after the end of World War II.

In that year I became a disciple of Master Kinoshita Jakugen, and started to learn Buddhism from Heart Sutra. From the following spring, as I entered the Hieizan Junior high school in Otsu, Shiga prefecture, I was moved to Jisho-in Temple (current Kanju-in Temple) in Sakamoto, in the foothills of Mount Hiei, which Master Kinoshita ran, where my Buddhism training started in earnest.

There I lived with a senior disciple. We were requested to do all of the housework on our own—cleaning, laundry, cooking, and preparing baths. All of these were hard for me, for I had been living without any need of doing such things in my past days.

My special challenge was water drawing. As I already suspected, there was no tap water in the temple, so we needed to go to the river to collect water. Not only for cooking, but a mere bath needs a surprisingly large amount of water. This meant we were almost endlessly shuttling between the river and the temple carrying the water bucket, which was hopelessly heavy.

Two of us supported a horizontal pole, one at each end with the bucket suspended in the center. Since I was shorter than my senior disciple, whenever the bucket swayed along with our steps, water from inside the bucket splashed onto me. On chilly days in winter, I was shivering with cold because of being wet to the skin. Still, it was much better that it was only water that splashed onto me. Much better than the night soil shall we say?

In those days there was no sewer system there. Yet it was natural that we had something daily aggregated in privies—as long as we were alive. Then, the issue was how to treat this waste—we collected it manually, and again, the two of us, the senior and me carried a bucket to transport it to the cesspool. And just like the water in the water bucket, whenever the bucket swayed as we transported it, the contents splashed onto the shorter one, me, which this time was a big deal.

Every evening when I prepared for the bath, I saw the lights in the town. "There is a station. If I go there to catch a train, I can go back to Kyoto to see Mom." I always stared at the light filled with such a feeling. I say my training days were never easy days, but at the same time I would say many times that they surely gave me the great gifts: patience, strong will to pursue, and the revelation of how much we owe to our parents. And these are surely my irreplaceable possessions forever mine, even if I went completely bankrupt tomorrow.

*The work expressing training days: "Look! There it is, mother, the first evening star!"
(Ikenobo Exhibition, in the memory of 60 years succession of the Headmaster)*

 Here Again

I recall myself as an ordinary boy who by nature had no special interest in *ikebana*. Thanks to my father teaching me much about trees and flowers, I do have some interest in botanical matters, but I have no wondrous anecdotes to recall in praise of some *ikebana* child prodigy. I wish I had some story to tell, but to tell you the truth I was really, just an average kid. It was not until some years later, that I embarked on the *ikebana* practices after I started living in a temple to do my Buddhist training.

After classes when I was returning to the temple where I lived, my friends would often joyfully discuss where next to go to hang out together, to play baseball or whether to go to the shore of Biwa lake. I would enthusiastically join the discussion and envisage the plans unfolding in reality, but then soon after returning to the temple, someone would always visit me—
"Here, I brought your flowers!"

It was the voice of the florist bringing flowers for my daily evening *ikebana* practice.
Surprisingly, he came each and every day. He always brought a single kind of flower for "*isshuike*" (*Shoka* style

using a single kind of material) or two kinds of flower for "*nishuike*" (*Shoka* style using two kinds of material), and it was my daily routine to practice *Shoka* using "*matagi*," a forked branch, at that time a method not yet in common use, instead of "*kenzan.*"

Soon after I started my *ikebana* practice, I started living with my *ikebana* teacher, Ms. Kazu Fujii who was born in 1905, the same year of birth with my mother. I remember her telling me before she went shopping to: "Finish up your *ikebana* work." My time with Ms. Fujii lasted almost ten years.

Although I understood I needed to be disciplined with *ikebana*, I was at the age where being in the company of friends was a complete preoccupation for me. Each day after managing to finish *ikebana* practice, I would rush out to see my friends, but it was so soon after, that the sun went down, and I had to go home again. On the way back I always wished I could play more the next day, but then the image of the florist came into my mind, too.

Somehow I did not neglect my flower practice, not even once. "It was because you loved *ikebana*" I can hear you saying, but no, this was not true. Put simply and honestly, it did not occur to me to neglect it.

I sometimes think back to the times in my younger days when I noticed the florist had arrived, I would mutter with a sigh, "Here he is again..."

At the ceremony for entering Buddhist training in September 1945, dressed in the robes of a Buddhist priest for the first time.

Respect for Another

Among other reasons, I respect a person who can do what I cannot, regardless of age or gender.

From my younger days, I have been trying various things that have aroused my interest. Among the things I have obtained licenses to drive, operate, or practice, these include large motorcycles, ships, amateur radio, skiing, diving, water skiing, ink painting, *haiku*, and more—and in putting this list down on paper, I flatter myself as relatively versatile and skillful. Some activities I came to enjoy so much that I improved significantly despite being less than enthusiastic in the beginning. There were others that I soon gave up on because of difficulties greater than I expected. But either way it is interesting to experience something on one's own in order to pick up some unique difficulty or quirky behavior not seen superficially. Of course, there are some areas that I will forever be excluded from anyway, and which finally made me aware of some of my limitations. Through such experiences, I have found new goals to aspire to achieve.

For example I am interested in architecture, which naturally makes me imagine aspects of interior design. So I may be able to do something like designing a house. But what happens if I am to actually construct this house? —obviously, at this point I will throw my hands in the air...

This is not only the case with the house of course. Everything necessary for our lives is in some way via another person's hands. We would never have seen automobiles running down the streets if I was responsible for inventing and developing them.

Typically if I take a look to my own Ikenobo building work, it is without doubt equipped with tap water and electricity. When we turn on the faucet we can soon access water, be it cold or hot, and we can enjoy a nice comfortable temperature both in winter and summer. When we give the toilet a flush, perhaps we don't spare much thought about where the water comes from and goes to, and in what ways, but sometimes this comes to my mind.

Civilization is relevant to every scene of our daily lives. In other words, people cannot live without being helped by others.

On the other hand, we see examples of animals that have solitary existences. Basically they live alone, breed alone, and die alone. Some can, or have to, stand up soon after they are born, and their entire concern is how to protect themselves from their enemies. We can grow up in protected surroundings, and are given many chances to survive, but that is not the case for the solitary animal. We can be treated for and survive the injuries we sustain, but for our animal, the slightest carelessness would lead to death.

We often say "Thank you" to express gratitude for a benefit or courtesy directly bestowed on us from someone near to us. Yet with this expression I would like to represent my respect and gratitude to our many ancestors who have produced numerous and varied utilities, equipment and systems that now support our lives. This is why I respect every person, professional or otherwise who can do what I cannot.

No one can live alone. Our lives are supported by many others, and in that way we live "thanks to everyone." This is what we should always keep in mind. It would be a dull life without someone's achievements to inspire you would it not?

 Individuality

Suppose I have two rings, one with a small diamond and the other with a large zirconia stone. If I were to say "Take whichever one you like," without telling you which is which, what would you do?

It is true that a few may choose the zirconia ring. The point is of course that you can easily decide if you know the difference in brightness between the two, but I do not mean to degrade the zirconia ring.

I am somewhat interested in how people choose the accessories that they wear. Sometimes I see a woman on the train wearing zirconia earrings which I find stylish. While at other times I see a woman on the same train wearing a gorgeous diamond necklace but it does not strike me as suitable for her.

I do not mean that I care about the type of jewelry or its price when looking at accessories. I think on it more when believe I can understand the sentiments of the person wearing it. Most women have many accessories and among them they choose to wear something they like at that time and on that day according to the way they are feeling. So I feel it is interesting to try to guess their intention and taste, and also what motivated them to choose that particular accessory item. Perhaps the one who knows what suits her best looks striking due to her ability to effuse confidence, and so it catches one's attention naturally.

Perhaps again, this is true when applying the final touches to an *ikebana* work. Students create a work according to their sensibilities as they wish. But some teachers pull out all the flowers the student did during the final stages. If this happens, then it is quite likely that the student will be at least disappointed but at worst completely dejected. The work rebuilt from the beginning by the teacher is then work by that teacher, which would be as if it were a demonstration by the teacher.

In my opinion, those final stages should never be addressed in such a one-sided approach. It should start by first accepting and understanding the sensibility of the original creator and the creator's individuality. Based on this, I would then try to find how to advance the student's progress, make corrections as far as if there are any non-compliances to the rules, but at the same time assist in the pursuit of individuality by directly showing an expression example—that is what the teachers should do.

Back to accessories... Even if they were purchased in a fabulous brand shop, or casually bought from a nearby shop, those accessories are something might well express what the wearer is disclosing about herself. If she looks nice with it, I would say "It looks wonderful on you," and if not I would just say nothing, rather than saying "You shouldn't be wearing that, it does not suit you at all," which would be none of my business!

I have opportunities to look at many works in exhibitions. Every work should have something attractive. By evaluating these attractive points, and then offering a new perspective, students will realize that they really are making progress.

Temple with Swans

When you visit Rokkakudo, you will find several swans in the pond of the precinct. Some visitors are surprised simply by the size of these birds, especially up close, and others may question why these migratory birds are staying here. Further, there might be some that consider that they are captives and they don't fly because their wings have been clipped. While walking around the precinct, I often hear people talk. Most people, however, are awed by the presence of swans.

The actual reason why the swans are here is, to tell you the truth, because there is insufficient space for them to take off. Smaller birds such as ducks can quickly take off without a take-off run first, but swans, with their large body size, need a long distance to get up to speed for take-off, just like a jumbo jet. Sometimes the swan in our pond tries to start the run, but it does not work and ends up looking somewhat halfhearted—just a show for the visitors.

At first, the food intended for the swans was often taken by sparrows. If I place a feed box on the ground, sparrows will quickly arrive to dine. So now I place the base of the feed box with its entrance protruding a little toward the water surface, and I put a curtain over the entrance that also lies on the water surface. This means that the swans with their long necks can access the food from the pond side of the box but the sparrows cannot, for they are just limited by the water surface.

I have carefully considered and planned what food and what quantity to give, but the swans often seem to eat the grass growing around the pond, too. There is a weeping willow on the pond side at the Dojo Building entrance, which they also seem to enjoy grazing.

The weeping willow with its graceful falling canopy sways gently in the breeze. The ends of the branches pulling down to the ground just like an ink brush is also lily. Yet, once I found the weeping willow just beside the Dojo Building entrance trimmed in a straight bobbed style. Nobody cuts a willow like that, so I wondered why it was so, and before long I found out. It was a deed done courtesy of our swans. As the swans ate the new willow buds, all the ends of the branches were gone and so it became the bobbed willow. They are neatly cut straight at the upper height limit of a swan's stretching neck plus beak.

This is what I finally gave up on trying to correct. So, yet again, I shall be looking at the bobbed weeping willow for another year.

A swan eating the new buds of a weeping willow

How Teachers Should Be

In the Ikenobo Central Training Institute, there is a teacher whose class is always full of students. Besides his technique in *ikebana*, what attracts so many students to his classes are his expansive lectures. It is first of all fun, and what's more it is compelling, such that the students desire to be led further into his *ikebana* world, and they always look forward to the next lecture.

A basic question should be asked now. What is the meaning of "teaching"? Well, I see it as not merely disseminating knowledge, but also giving the students a route to acquire the capacity to learn independently.

For example, in Ikenobo we classify plant materials into three categories; "*ki* (tree materials)," "*kusa* (grassy materials)," and "*tsuyomono* (plant materials that have characteristics of both "*ki*" as well as "*kusa*"). In teaching these classifications to the students, if we just tell them "Pine is '*ki*', Iris is '*kusa*', and Hydangea is '*tsuyomono*', " this actually does not mean we are teaching. It is just a list of names and their classifications. Rather, teaching gives the students the ability to classify on their own. The learn *how* to classify.

"*Ki* are something that keep on developing over the years which is evident by their growth rings. *Kusa* grow anew every year with its new buds. *Tsuyomono* then are the remaining items, in which the inside of their stems are hollow without growth rings and do not wither in winter like grassy materials."

By explaining the reasoning like this, students will understand the criteria of the classification, enabling them to judge it for themselves. This will take them a step up in their training.

Keep on giving them tips, that is, clues to answer their questions, as to why something is the way it is, how it should be recognized, and what will happen next. Then the students become excited in anticipation of the logic and explanation that follows. If they experience such excitement and satisfaction enough to realize that they are actually making progress, they would surely spend more time with that teacher. Just like a premium restaurant, even if it is a challenge to reach in a remote place, it will still be sought by many customers.

Moreover, the teacher I quoted above gives the students assignments. Sometimes the students have to read a particular book, and answer questions in the next class. This is wonderful I think, because a lesson is not only that given by teachers, but also one in which students should be requesting answers too. The students study hard at home to prepare for the next class in which they might be pointed to answer the teacher's question. And surely their efforts are rewarded by gaining confidence.

So my point is we teachers should give students a boost to request more training, more opportunities to learn, so that they can realize how much they have improved, which will surely move them. Also, I hope all teachers will respect each student, and his or her sensitivities, to promote their strengths.

Just reading the tutorials and telling the students to imitate the teacher's work doesn't move many students. Explaining the basics, encouraging their uniqueness, and leading them to follow their own paths in the future, this is the way. To enable this, touch-ups, where the teacher is forced impose his interpretation on a student's work would be a last resort.

Just because, since old times, a disciple would always follow the *teaching* of a master, not his work.

🌼 Beauty of Life

My most favorite time—is a time when I am watching nature alive. It never bores me no matter how long I watch.

In the Ikenobo Building hall, there are many animals. In the room where I spend most of my time, I have several horned owls. Instead of a bird cage, I have made a space like a separate room along one wall, partitioned with transparent acrylic sheet in which the owls can live. You may wonder why I chose horned owls. One reason is that the owls are a lucky mascot, but I like them because they are quiet. They stand still during the daytime as they are nocturnal animals. Even when still, they look just beautiful. I have carefully positioned the several perches in their area to beautifully and effectively display the owls. The bird cage in the lobby of the first floor is also designed with similar intentions, as if they are playing a role of showing "a moving picture."

The room also contains insect specimens, each of which carries a unique and different pattern from the others even though on first inspection they look the same—beautiful like a premium chocolate assortment. Yet my first choice is always the beauty of living things. Not only the momentous impression left by each animal, with the daily changes that I can see in them—new hairs growing in a specific season, or developing body size—these observations never bore me. And through such events and scenes their lives spin into the yarn of nature. I am greatly impressed and this gives me inspiration to create my *ikebana* works.

This is all the same with people. If we pursue beauty only superficially, a woman with the most beautiful looks is really a Mannequin. They all have outstanding facial looks, the best proportions, and are decorated in the most gorgeous clothes. But no one will seriously fall in love with a Mannequin girl. Why? Because it has no heart. We as human beings fall in love with other living human beings. Since we are alive, since we have hearts, we comprehend each other intuitively.

This again is the same with *ikebana*. Living is the most important point. Being alive, *ikebana* work is in a constant state of flux, too. It is proof of life, where the life dwells on and on. Because *ikebana* is living, it can move the hearts of those who look at it. This is something that artificial flowers can never do.

This is why I would rather take in the natural view of outdoors, rather than look at a great landscape painting in a room. How the trees and flowers put on their displays all through the seasons. I am so glad when I find a "*yoroshiki omokage* (beauty of the original impression given us by each plant)" that my father taught me.

Horned owls standing still in daytime, as if they were the characters in a painting.

My Syria Report

As I so often feel the urge to travel to many places officially or privately, I have been to so many countries and regions. When telling people about such exploits, I am often asked "What is the country that impressed you the most?" My answer is of course "Syria."

On February 24 and 25 in 1997, the first *ikebana* exhibition was held in Syria at the Damascus Sheraton hotel in Damascus, the capital of Syria, sponsored by the Japanese Embassy of Syria. With this exhibition as the main event, the Ikenobo tour was planned as a tour of several countries including Syria, Jordan, Italy, Holland, and France.

I have attended *ikebana* exhibitions and demonstrations concerned with the embassy of various countries many times, but this time I was a little nervous. I recognized this was an area of political instability, and that we, the other professors and myself, were required to behave with restraint and caution. Still, this was just some information I gleaned from the media, such as TV or newspapers, and which did not resonate with my real feelings.

Once we arrived at the airport in Syria, we were to move to the hotel and the embassy using the pickup bus, but what surprised me was that we were meticulously chaperoned by an army escort. Perhaps this was because we were invited by the Japanese Embassy, but this was a chance for me to observe up close something of military life. As my home is in Kyoto, I had never had any experience of a military presence including during World War II, as Kyoto was spared from air raids. Looking at the beautiful mosque through the bus window, I had no choice but to simply take in and understand that the peace surrounding me can be fragile. Probably it was not only me but other people in Ikenobo who attended the tour were probably similarly affected even though no one said anything. That was the time I felt worried and uneasy about whether the people in this country would accept our *ikebana* favorably.

However I was totally betrayed by my worries once we started to work on our displays at the exhibition. Partly because the first *ikebana* was just such a fascinating sight for the curious, many Syrian people came to see even while we were preparing to work on *ikebana*, and of course the main exhibition was very successful.

Come to think of it, there should be no one that hates flowers. We often tell and hear the story about a soldier who was healed by a flower in a field during war. It was my fault that I almost lost my confidence in the power of *ikebana*, flowers and trees, led astray by a nervous feeling in an unusual environment.

As I noticed in a real natural sense that I was free from any nervousness after that. I came to my senses. We were still chaperoned by the army escort all through our stay in Syria, right up to the border to our next visiting country, Jordan, but that didn't make me tense any more. I was sure that any soldier would be our neighbor too, he who has the heart to love a flower.

Palmyra ruins in Syria. A part of these buildings was bombed and completely destroyed by a terrorist organization in 2015.

Memory of My Sense

As stated in the previous chapter, I often travel abroad either on business or privately. My passport pages are already filled with stamps from my countless travels, including all the extra pages I have asked to add for more travel.

My first journey abroad was the one to Hawaii. It was 1962, when overseas travel was not so commonplace. I was really excited by what was to be my first life-changing event, getting on an airplane to Hawaii.

I remember it was almost eight o'clock in the evening when we arrived at Honolulu airport. The Sun had already set, and it was so dark. The burning flame of the torch that welcomed us at the airport impressed me a lot, helping me to get in a tropical mood.

Settled in a hotel room after a long ride, I walked to the balcony to open the window. Suddenly then, warm air rushed in to wrap around me. There was the soft wind and some beating sound. Beyond the window there was an ocean. I pondered whether that sound came from the ocean as I listened to its comfortable repeating pattern for a while.

Next morning, as the daylight grew brighter, I looked outside. Then I knew what was making that comforting noise. It was the rustling sound of palm leaves. Beyond the window, it was that perfect familiar Hawaiian view that I had seen in pictures and on TV.

Memory is something mysterious I think. Every time I remember Hawaii, what comes to my mind is not the blue ocean or the abundant greenery, but the night, strictly speaking what I experienced on that night—the night air, the wind, and the smell. Rather than what I saw, what I felt is strongly embedded in my memory. When we see a picture of our sweet old times, we often quietly stare at the picture with feelings of our half-forgotten memory. Yet when we smell something old, our reaction is much stronger. Even before feeling that old and sweet memory, we are unconsciously brought back to "that time." The memory of our feeling is deep and strong, much deeper and stronger than we expect. I mean, our memory links more strongly to something invisible, rather than to the color or the shape. Even now, I clearly remember that night in Hawaii by the scent in the wind that I inadvertently had. And every time I visit Hawaii, I somehow try to find the air I experienced on that day.

After these experiences, I came to think I would like to express such memories of mine with *ikebana*. Time that greenery has experienced, the environment that cherished them, and the winds which blew around them—I strongly wanted to create a work in which the image of that greenery I have kept in my memory can be effectively expressed from within myself.

Not only *ikebana* as a form, but a work filling a space with memories of green. This is what I aim for. I hope this will also move the people who see the work, and become a work lasting in their hearts, longer than the pictures.

With the topic of "A Journey of the Heart," work expressing memories of Hawaii, the first country I visited.
(from "Ikenobo Ikebana 550th Year Celebration Special Memorial Exhibition")

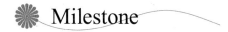# Milestone

Shofutai, the traditional method of Ikenobo, has a model to follow. Not only *ikebana* but other Japanese traditional cultures such as *"sado"* or *"knoh"* also possess such models or patterns to follow, and we all start the training from properly and faithfully adhering to the guides of these patterns. In *ikebana*, too, students can often be seen struggling to make the branches follow the proper pattern, and sometimes they may feel like blaming their materials as a reason for not attaining the good work they wish for. Still, once the teachers touch up such works, suddenly they see the proper pattern, at which time their respect for their teachers would rise.

In *ikebana*, we often select branches according to a pattern, whereby we try to find a suitable branch for a specific part, or find a branch of the most suitable thickness to integrate the materials into the pattern. Such an approach of *"kidori,"* branch selection, is quite important. Beginners tend to have difficulty in selecting an optimum combination, but gradually they do manage to learn and acquire a natural, harmonized *"kidori"* technique. Then they are going to jump up to the next step of their training. At this point they are requested to look at the pattern from a new perspective.

To clear this step, I like them to look at greenery rooted in the ground. Wild plants stretching their branches and leaves as their properties request are spontaneous on the one hand, and on the other hand cluttered. Yet this is how they actually are. So the students would move to the further step, in which they are requested to face greenery with the viewpoint of finding a pattern within their true manifestations.

To explain this, I would say it is that they are required to have the critical eye that selects which branch to leave and which to cut out. Looking at an entire plum tree, for example, they need to know how it can be a *Shoka* work, selecting which branches to trim. Which branch possesses the strength of life, which branch pursues sunlight, and which part expresses its specific character most impressively. Based on such a process, once they judge the branches in front of them using their senses, then they can trim either the unnecessary branches or ones whose functions are overlapping.

The *ikebana* works based on this process, dependent on the sensitivity, tend to show characteristics more effectively than those simply following and relying on the patterns.

And since they express the uniqueness of their creator, they give an opportunity for introspection, clarifying what kind of appreciation the creator has, what moves him or her the most. Then gradually the most basic pattern reveals its creator's character.

In the beginning the patterns are used milestones pointing towards the height of *ikebana*. If, however we depend on these waypoints too much, we run the risk of confusing the milestones with the destination, the pattern as the purpose, thus losing sight of the true goal. Just as a milestone is only a guide, not a goal for a traveler, so is the pattern for any creator. The purpose of *ikebana* is never the pattern itself. Keep the patterns and go beyond them to where each creator should find his or her own taste. This is the real joy of *ikebana*.

Each of our *ikebana* professors with their long careers has found their own taste. If one with a good appreciation takes a look at their works, he or she can tell who the work belongs to without needing to check a name tag. I really hope that all the students will walk down the long path of *ikebana* with the guide of the great milestones of the patterns but at the same time in a spirit of no constraints. Because one of the best compliments I think is as below;

"I know this *is* your work."

🌸 Message from *Ayu*

Ayu, the Japanese sweetfish, is my favorite fish that I need on the table every season. I go to buy this tasty fish routinely every season, just as an annual event. In the market, I would definitely choose one swimming in the water, rather than one neatly laid out in a package. Fresher *ayu* is much tastier of course, but what is more it is easier to separate the fish meat from the bones and the small bones are easier to remove. As it is often known as sweetfish, *ayu* is wonderful grilled with salt or just in a raw, *sashimi* style.

Ayu is also familiar in paintings. The summer paintings typical in *"kakejiku"* are of the fish swimming swiftly amongst new greenery, which is something very popular in the hot seasons with their cool impressions. The bodies of *ayu* look slender and smooth which is typical of freshwater fish, and their ripe lips or stubby faces look just friendly and lovely.

Still, this fish also has some traits that one cannot foresee from its outlook. Its strong territoriality which is in turn used in lure fishing, or its strong physical capacity that allows them to commute between their birth river and the ocean, are some good examples showing their inner strength hidden by their mild external impression.

And it is the pictures of them swimming that impressed me most. They are just swimming in the river, but convey such a strong impression. It is not the physical strength the fish possess I am referring to here; it is the strength I can get from its attitude toward life. *Ayu* swim according to the water flow, but at the same time they keep on swimming without drifting off course. Such style evokes in me the feeling of strength more than any other.

If *ayu* has any will, the purpose would be just to survive and to preserve its species. Their swimming style to pursue such a goal is simple, strong, and therefore beautiful.

We humans can make a detour or sometimes even lose our original purpose by being influenced by another's opinion or swayed by unwieldy amounts of information. It is hard, harder than expected, to be strong enough to hold ourselves on a particular course, to be defiant of circumstances.

In our lives sometimes we have to choose many other ways other than making a decision in a simple, graceful manner or even maintaining our inner strength. And this is why I feel the sense of beauty in someone who can do that. What I mean is not the beauty of appearance again, but the beauty of attitude, something coming from within. Such beauty never fades through the ages, indeed, it can be refined over the accumulated years of experiences.

Of course people are different from the fish. Yet why don't we take a long breath and just imagine the *ayu*'s swimming style, when we are about to lose ourselves or when we are being forced to make a quick and tough decision? It would surely give us a hint, asking ourselves whether our style in the situation was *beautiful* or not.

"Ayu" drawn by Tekison Uda, Owned by Ikenobo Headquarters

Keeping the Soil for *Ikebana*

There is something inevitably essential to *ikebana*, and that is Nature, and the vegetation nurtured by Nature. I say this not from the physical logic where we never can do *ikebana* without using vegetation itself as the material, but from my concept that we should know how plant life thrives in Nature in order to revitalize and appreciate it in *ikebana*.

Such fruitful Nature is always behind the sense of beauty that we Japanese are now famous for—the loving and cherishing of the various natural elements in each season. And, the beauty which dwells at the very basis of *ikebana*, one of the Japanese traditional cultures, is represented by the life of vegetation and Nature it is part of.

I once had a chance to talk to some of our devotees who were attending our national convention, on the subject of "How we can prepare fertile soil for *ikebana*." The words "fertile soil for *ikebana*" I used did not simply mean those fundamental practices, but also implied the perception in which everyone comes to know the reason why a certain work of *ikebana* is regarded as beautiful, and moreover the basic social awareness upon which *ikebana* is widely accepted. In other words, the "soil" here is the comprehension of the true image of natural vegetation, the very root of *ikebana*'s beauty, through the five senses, and the ability to discern in which part of the *ikebana* work such beauty is expressed.

Now I have the unmistakable feeling that such *ikebana* soil is less fertile than it used to be. The progress of urbanization and with it the destruction of nature has been making a critical impact on the environment, and wild flowers, such as golden lace or Chinese bellflower, the typical autumn herbs in Japan, are now classed as endangered species, such as they are, dependent on their native growing locations.

Campion used to be a typical flower used as decoration in the *Tanabata* festival. Yet currently the original species is already extinct, and the ones we can see now as "campion" are strictly a related species. In Ikenobo the *Rikka* style of work using campion has been a seasonal routine for the *Tanabata* festival, but currently we have to depend on related species instead. It is my regret that the Japanese culture of customs such as *Tanabata* is fading from public awareness due to the extinction of certain species.

We can see another good example in the famous *haiku*:

"Asagaoya Tsurube Torarete Moraimizu"
(Morning glory has taken over the rope of well-bucket;
I must find water from elsewhere.)

Kaga-no Chiyojo

Although this *haiku* is very popular, many of our young generation do not know what the well was like in the first place. They cannot imagine the situation, for they don't know what *"tsurube"* is either. Further, they have of course no idea that the vines of morning glory wind counterclockwise when viewed from above. This *haiku* depicts the situation, where the author goes to collect water from a well, and finds the morning glory vines are wound around the rope of the well bucket, so the author visits another place to ask for water, instead of removing the vines from the rope. Not only do we hear the representation of the event, but also the implication that the author greatly cherishes morning glory and is being kind because of this.

I mean, the background of *haiku*, the ordinary situation depicted in *haiku* is no longer ordinary in the present day, and the popular herbs used in those days are already something quite rare and special. What is happening here is that the Japanese traditional sense of beauty that has long been nurtured in its fruitful natural environment is little by little slipping away. This should be nothing short of crisis for *ikebana*, just as for the shortages in vegetation materials, due to environmental impact.

Again, the beauty of Ikenobo *ikebana* is totally based on the style of greenery in nature. As for those of us within *ikebana*, what can we do to preserve it and show it to the rest of the world as a sustainable Japanese traditional culture. If the changes occurring over time inevitably destroy nature, we must maintain our efforts to protect nature from our changes. Not only bemoaning the situation where the soil for *ikebana* is becoming poor, we have to lead the actions for developing an environment in which the younger generations can cultivate the Japanese sense of beauty. Truly, people are moved strongly by what they actually experience with their five senses.

Knowing the Genuine Article

Looking up the Japanese word "*koyasu*" (enrich, fertilize) in a dictionary gives the meaning as follows: to fertilize lands, to give nutrition, to fill out, enrich or entertain, empower with knowledge or appreciation.

Although an unfavorable application such as "enrich or fatten one's wallet" is also possible, the word "*koyasu*" basically means enriching, and enriching anything in our life, such as enriching our sense of taste or appreciation, means intrinsic enrichment of our lives. I don't mean to recommend a luxury life; I only believe the experience of knowing 'the genuine article' can enrich our lives.

The benefits of advanced technology we have gained in these current times may, I anticipate, deprive us of the chance of knowing what is real and what are genuine articles or events. Paintings painted by hand have gradually been converted into printed reproductions, the original sources of songs or instrumental pieces have been changed into CD's, and the real scenery into imaged pictures. Everything is or can be reproduced in superb quality of course, but still, they are not perfectly same as the originals.

Once we actually see a famous painting with our own eyes which we saw before on TV or in magazines many times, we may be suddenly struck, and realize the reason why the painting is so valued and widely admired. Original paintings carry with them those real touches resulting from the breath of the painter or his/her body temperature. Traces of the paint brush that has overlaid color so many times, the shade finally determined after mixing so many different colors— even though it "looks" the same, the printed material, based on the same numerical values after analysis and coordination of inks, the original painting stands before us, and talks to our hearts and spirits on a completely different level. This is also the case for music. For example, original human voices we enjoy at concerts can convey much, not only to our ears but also in other physical sensations, such as subtle vibrations in the sounds of voices or instruments, resonances due to variations of temperature or humidity, let alone the real physical condition of the singers. Also, although a high-precision image can clearly catch a beautiful moment, we cannot directly feel the ever-changing light or breeze which we can enjoy while experiencing real scenery "on location" so to speak.

Even a most perfect imitation cannot be real, and the VR technology allowing us to feel as if we are actually in a remote place can only give us a *virtual* experience—just alike, but not the reality.

I once heard some words from an architect: "If you want to design a premium hotel, you need to stay in a premium hotel yourself." Besides the definition of what is premium, I understand he mentioned that the knowledge and the experience is totally different. He implies that staying in a premium hotel, even though it might be a slightly big jump, can be a career investment for future architects. And I think it must be essential to know the definitions of premium and high quality, if not to possess things with such attributes.

Sensitivity is somewhat based on natural character, and cannot always be easily acquired. Yet some of it can be brought out by enriching our appreciation and evaluation. The process of enrichment is, I believe, to take in as many genuine, original, real and worthy experiences as possible.

The pieces evaluated by many people as masterpieces should have some reason to attract us. A premium exhibit should have a reason to make it premium. Experiencing a many great exhibits, listening to them, tasting them, accumulating impressions or sensations with our own five senses, will refine our sensitivity. In this context, children should, rather than adults, experience the real and genuine as far as possible. Even though they may not understand at that time, they should unconsciously start cultivating seeds of fruitful sensitivity. As we say in our proverb "What is learned in the cradle is carried to the grave," the door of sensitivity opened in childhood can never be closed for the rest of one's life. Nurturing sensitivity is an individual task for each child, but we have to first open the door for them.

As the Headmaster of Ikenobo *ikebana*, I feel strongly about the necessity to open the door of sensitivity, which in turn results in *ikebana*'s root spirits—infusing new life into the vegetation materials, welcoming the viewers with hospitality by the help of *ikebana*, and cherishing the natural greenery.

Some young people these days do not care if they see artificial flowers used as decoration in an authentic Japanese inn or even in a Buddhist altar. Perhaps they accept them, as long as such artificial flowers are in some way perfectly beautiful just as real flowers are. Yet my opinion is different. Living in Japan, full of elegant beauty with its four seasons, I wish them to have much keener sensitivity. I would like to leave a future to our children where they can naturally have the real, genuine experiences to enrich a genuine sensitivity.

The Promise of the Flower Buds

In my life, I have seen so many days, good and bad. I was born in 1933, I remember what Japan was like in World War II, and saw with my own eyes the economic growth after the War that invigorated the entire country. I also experienced that crazy bubble boom in a buoyant mood, and in complete contrast, the stagnation after it burst. I have been given many chances to go abroad, so for such various differences in each country, not only Japan, too, I have firsthand knowledge and experience to some extent.

When I was a child, it was a time when everything was in short supply. We all had to learn to be patient in every way. When the knees of my trousers were worn through and torn, my mother used to mend them with patches. Not only me, but everybody was disheveled, children were snotty nosed, and everybody wore ad hoc patched clothing. If my mother were alive now, she would be wide-eyed with surprise at the young people walking around in jeans with purpose-made holes ripped here and there for a cool look.

Such experiences of mine truly bring home to me the happiness of present times. An air conditioner keeps us comfortable in any season, all through the year, and even the toilet seat is nicely warm everywhere. In the coming ten years, perhaps we will have an even more comfortable life at hand.

It must be true, though, that the perspective is therefore quite different between these two; those who have been taking the gift of civilization and technology for granted, and those who once experienced the days of shortage and pain—like me. It is accordingly unavoidable that teachers have different values or sensibilities from their students and of course from the students of them.

Nevertheless, I believe that different values and sensibilities can coexist, where no one can judge or criticize the other for being totally opposite in some way, for example. It is not only the matter of whether either of the two is right and correct. What is needed is mutual respect, freedom from judgment of the other by only using one's own scale.

We can long for our good old days and even tell stories about such great memories to younger people, but if we stick only to our past we will have no hope for the future.

I myself do not speak about the past to my two grandchildren, such things as the difficult times we experienced. If I was asked to, perhaps I would talk, but rather I would like them to directly experience a great variety of things with their own eyes and ears just as I did.

In Ikenobo, we regard the flower buds as the future, the blooming flowers as present, and the fruits as past. Speaking of cherry blossoms for example, full bloom flowers are indeed quite magnificent, and falling petals also have a great attraction. Still, my favorite of all are the flower buds because I find enormous potential in the young buds just at the time they are about to bloom in the coming season.

Flowers and fruits are also important with each having its specific role. When we are in the 'flowering stage' we are required to live, much as a flower, and no matter whether we are budding or a fruit, it would be the same. We always need to strive for in full stroke, in each every stage of our life.

We all know that we were once tiny buds, too. Even if the buds of the current times bloom to develop into new, completely different flowers from what we knew, no one would deny they are equally precious and valuable. Why can't we bring them up then, believing in their promise?

Walking Together

Remaining essentially unchanged for a long time, maintaining our presence with certain continued style, and spending time together over life times. These are some of the very special gifts that we hardly ever attain to our complete satisfaction. So many remarks to remember, so many quotes, so much wisdom, these all tell us about how transitory all of worldly things are. I too, have been too stunned to speak by the sudden change forced upon me, the impact of the sudden loss of my father, and again when I lost my mother and brother even though in those cases I half expected them, nevertheless the finality hit me no less severely.

Because I lost my father during my younger years, and soon after I left my mother to start Buddhist training alone, I think my bond with my parents I had determined, was not very strong. Looking back to my formative years, I was once too sensitive and naive for the word "family." During those times I tried not to think about my loneliness or uneasy feelings because I missed my parents so much. Instead I tried to throw myself into Buddhist training and even more into *ikebana* training.

The other side of the coin was that, however, in those days I was in a perfect situation for devoting myself to the world of religion and *ikebana*, where there was literally nothing else at all to distract me. And this was because the disciples from my grandfather's and my father's days had long been taking care of me and Ikenobo.

The disciples of my parents age supported me when I was still young, guarded me, and shared the pleasure of nurturing daughter just as if she were their own grandchild. The disciples of my own age were always approaching me in *ikebana* with the same friendly attitude. And the younger disciples. I want to say students gave me the joy of watching their growth and development. I arrogantly felt that they were all part of a precious family of *mine*, those of my age spending their time with me.

Like everyone else, I felt that the two huge earthquakes that hit, one in Hanshin Awaji and the other in north eastern Japan were just too terrible to contemplate. Our main institute in Kyoto had almost no damage, but there were many disciples in affected locations. I was only worrying for *my family* taking the same *ikebana* path even though they were actually in need of help, which was my great frustration. I noticed again, that our *ikebana* exhibitions and numerous events we had been doing were something

I can never take for granted. I blamed myself for almost forgetting this; for I must have been someone, more than anyone, who should be so familiar with the fragileness of such ordinary happiness.

After my countless thoughts, I went back to a single idea: all I wanted was to get back my disciples and their usual training days as soon as possible. So I moved toward this. I prepared support for their training and delivered this material to them as quickly as I could. I thought about them getting back their usual days with *ikebana* and that achieving this would be the restoration of my family, all together again, walking along the *ikebana* path. Tangible things can be damaged or lost so easily any day. On the other hand, the *ikebana* skill, the *ikebana* path we have been walking together is never impaired or lost. As long as they have materials for *ikebana*, this can move forward. Through *ikebana*, we can connect with other *families* also walking the *ikebana* path. I hope everyone will remember this.

Not only for these two heavy earthquakes, but also for the other setbacks too, I have not mentioned much in the past. I refrained from mentioning them because sometimes eloquent words are glamorized to such a point that they give an unexpectedly hollow impression, falling far short of the intention. Probably I am not going to speak loud about those tragedies. So this is one of my special chances to express my feelings toward my disciples. My disciples are my precious family, members of a huge *ikebana* family who once supported me so much when my usual days had collapsed. Some of them are probably still suffering from their wounds. Although among the things I imagine one thing stands out, and that is that we are daily, continuously, inescapably imperiled by some kinds of disasters. Still I want my family to depend on me. For I have determined myself to guard and cherish my *family* and *ikebana*, my two precious treasures for the rest of my life.

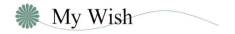 My Wish

In Ikenobo we have so many disciples all over Japan, and in the world. It is so impressive to me that this *Ikebana*, which had such humble beginnings in a small temple in Kyoto, has grown in the intervening 550 years to what it now. The records left in Ikenobo gave me literally countless names of disciples including some well-known and others not. This great number of people, whose faces or personalities I have no way of knowing, have been handed on Ikenobo *ikebana* with a part of, or even most of their lives. Until the present times, many disciples of Ikenobo have been walking along with Headmasters. How precious a thing it is, I stop to think.

Recently *ikebana* schools are said to be receiving decreasing numbers of disciples. One reason would be perhaps the broad reaches of people's taste. For example, in the past if someone was fond of flowers, he or she would have no other choice but to first learn *ikebana*. Yet currently there are many other alternative activities. There is flower arrangements, gardening, and art flowers, where he or she cannot just depend on *ikebana* anymore. The taste or specialty has been changed a lot, and divided into more specialized areas.

The people pursuing *ikebana*, and especially Ikenobo *ikebana*, have probably chosen it from numerous options they may have had. I must then seriously take their serious choice. What do they request in selecting the traditional culture? What can they take from *ikebana*, something they cannot take from flower arrangements or gardening? After contemplation, I reached an idea that it must be related with some concept of *"do,"* a long "way" to go.

As you may know, *ikebana* belongs the world of *"do,"* a "way," where people would often call it as *"kado."* Not only *kado*, we have many other *"do"* worlds such as *sado*, *shodo*, *kendo*, or *judo*. Masters of such *"do"* are somewhat filled with confidence, with their attitude sophisticated and simplified. This *"do"* world equally request the trainees to exercise for both technical and mental development. In other words, even the highest skill, if not accompanied with a sound and noble philosophy, cannot be evaluated or respected.

To those who started walking along the way of *"do,"* with aspirations of being one of the sophisticated masters, I would like to emphasize again, that you are also one of those endless points that eventually configure the continuous history of this respectful tradition. Indeed, numerous points connect and linked together to finally find themselves as an unbroken line of the "*do*" tradition.

It is necessary to look for future applicants for our future sake. Yet I would rather prefer caring for the current disciples I have now. What I wish is that they realize the true happiness and satisfaction from their learning experience in *ikebana*. Not only their progress in the skill or technique, but more than that, their confidence and feeling of fulfillment in which they can truly feel their lives have been enriched and fruited by the *ikebana* experience—that is nothing but my joy. I never doubt that one single fruitful life would so surely bring the productive lives of many followers.